Table of contents

American Medical Association
Physicians dedicated to the health of America

P. John Seward, MD
Executive Vice President

James F. Rappel
Group Vice President

Larry Jellen
Vice President, Marketing

M. Frances Dyra
Director, Product Line Development

Editorial staff

Patricia Dragisic
Managing Editor

Steven Michaels
Senior Editor

Robin Fitzpatrick Husayko
Editor

Debra A. Smith
Editorial Assistant

Acknowledgments

Larry S. Goldman, MD
Department of Mental Health, AMA

Ellen Hughes
Writer

Herb Hinkelman
Designer

Depression

Living with and treating the disorder

This book is intended to help people who may have depression—and their families and friends—understand the symptoms and causes of this sometimes confusing disease. It explains the various therapies and medications that are used to treat depression.

This book also discusses what you can do to help a depressed person and how you can find the professional help he or she needs. Early detection and treatment of depression can limit the damage caused by this destructive disease and help a depressed person enjoy life again.

Depression is a disabling disease that affects millions of Americans—men, women, and children—regardless of race, income, or family background. It's one of the most common, most dangerous, and most treatable of all diseases.

Left untreated, depression can destroy families, careers, lives, and, all too often, can lead to suicide. But there is still reason for hope. With proper diagnosis and treatment, most people can control their depression and prevent its unpleasant symptoms from disrupting their daily lives.

What is depression?

Everyone has felt depressed from time to time. A death in the family, a failed romance, a lost job, a serious illness, or other life crisis will cause most people to feel sad, lonely, or down for a time. A period of grief or sadness is a normal reaction to such stressful events. It's even normal to feel "blah" sometimes for no special reason. However, it also is normal to recover after a short time and feel like yourself again.

When the blues don't go away—when sad, lonely, irritable, or weary feelings prevent getting on with life—you, or someone you know, may have the mood disorder called depression. A mood disorder is an extreme, persistent disruption of a person's usual emotional state.

Depression is a "whole body" illness—one that affects a person's physical health as well as how he or she feels, thinks, and behaves toward others. A person who has depression may have problems sleeping, eating, working, and getting along with friends.

Depression can cause many different kinds of unhappy feelings. A depressed person may cry all the time, be very fearful, have panic attacks, argue with friends and coworkers, lose self-confidence, even have hallucinations. On the other hand, he or she might feel numb; not really sad, but not happy either.

People who are depressed will often try to self-medicate their bad feelings with drugs or alcohol, which only makes matters worse. Alcohol is a depressant, the last thing a depressed person needs.

Depression can come on suddenly, seemingly for no reason, or be triggered by a stressful event. It can also grow slowly over months and years, gradually draining away happiness and hope.

It is important for a person who is depressed—and his or her family, friends, and coworkers—to understand that depression is a disease. A depressed person has not caused these feelings and cannot simply decide to snap out of it and stop being depressed.

Depression is a very common health problem, and it is frequently misunderstood. People who have this illness often are embarrassed to admit they are depressed and to seek help for what they may see as a character flaw or weakness. This may be the reason two thirds of all people who are depressed never seek professional help.

Weakness has nothing to do with depression. Trying to ignore these feelings only gives them time to grow. Depression is a physical disorder that causes chemical changes inside the brain.

These changes will not go away on their own. Recovery from depression may require psychotherapy, medication, or a combination of these or other treatments.

Are you—or a family member or friend—depressed?

Following is a brief description of various depressive disorders. If the symptoms seem familiar, read on to learn what you can do. There are several basic types of depression:

Major depression

Of the estimated 17.5 million Americans who are affected by some form of depression, about 9.2 million have major or clinical depression, the most severe form. It is also called unipolar disorder because the person's mood remains at one extreme or pole of emotion—a constantly depressed feeling.

Listed below are typical symptoms of major depression. Some people who have this disorder experience only a few symptoms, while others may have almost all these feelings. See your doctor if you have any of these symptoms. If you have recurrent thoughts about suicide or death, talk to your doctor immediately.

- feeling sad or anxious most of the day, every day
- losing interest in activities you once enjoyed, including sex
- losing weight (when not dieting) or gaining weight
- sleeping too much or too little or waking too early
- feeling drained of energy or physically slowed down
- feeling tired or weak all the time
- feeling worthless, guilty, or hopeless
- feeling irritable or restless all the time
- having trouble concentrating, making decisions, or remembering things
- having headaches, digestive disorders, or chronic pain that doesn't respond to medical treatment
- having repeated thoughts of suicide or death or actually making a suicide plan or attempt

Adjustment disorder

Some people react to a very stressful event—loss of a job, breakup of a marriage, accident or major illness—with serious symptoms of depression that pass within a few months and do not return. This condition, called an adjustment disorder with depressed mood, does not usually require treatment. However, if the symptoms do not pass, you may have a more serious disorder (such as major depression) that requires treatment.

Dysthymia

A milder, but more lasting form of depression, dysthymia can go untreated for years, draining happiness and energy from the person's life and from the lives of his or her family and friends.

Dysthymia is diagnosed when a person has a generally depressed mood for most of the day, more days than not, for a period of at least 2 years (1 year in a child).

A person who has dysthymia is unable to find any fun in life. He or she may be always pessimistic, guilt-ridden, irritable, easily hurt by others, or withdrawn. Dysthymia can make it difficult for a person to get along with others at home, at school, and at work.

Children who have dysthymia may often be irritable, cranky, difficult, generally sad, and have low self-esteem.

People with treatable dysthymia rarely seek medical help. Always depressed, they are usually unable to imagine feeling better. Friends, family members, and even doctors may sometimes assume the person is just gloomy or grouchy by nature.

Treatment of dysthymia, which may involve psychotherapy, drug treatment, or a combination of the two, can offer the person a whole new outlook on life. Psychotherapy changes a person's attitudes and behavior through talking.

Manic-depressive illness

Manic-depressive illness is also called bipolar disorder because of the way a person who has this form of depression will swing between opposite extremes or poles of emotion.

During a depressive phase, the person has symptoms of major depression (see list of symptoms above).

During a manic phase, the person may feel very happy, agitated, irritable, or energized. He or she may sleep very little, make all kinds of wild plans, or talk constantly.

Some of the difficult "high" symptoms in the manic phase of this disorder include:

- inappropriate displays of happiness or excitement
- inability to sleep (sometimes for days) or a decreased need for sleep
- a high energy level
- sudden irritability
- the need to talk constantly, often loudly

- wild, racing thoughts
- being easily distracted
- inflated ideas of self-importance
- sudden increase in sexual desire
- impaired judgment, such as making wild plans or going on buying sprees
- inappropriate or embarrassing social behavior
- taking dangerous risks

Some people with bipolar mood disorder will spend months in one phase or the other, while others will swing back and forth between the two phases. How low the depression or high the manic phase feelings go differs from person to person.

Manic depressive illness usually is treated with a mood-stabilizing drug such as lithium, which may be combined with antidepressant medication.

What causes depression?

Although there is no medical test for depression, research has discovered a link to an imbalance of chemical messengers that enable brain cells to communicate with each other (called neurotransmitters) in the brain and depression.

Heredity appears to play a role in the risk of depression. People who have a strong family history of depression are more likely to become depressed. However, many people who have a strong family history of depression are never troubled by a mood disorder, even when under constant stress.

Personality type also plays a role in the development of depression. People who are very pessimistic, have low self-esteem, and get easily stressed-out by their problems also are more likely to become depressed.

Often, depression is triggered by a stressful event, such as the death of a loved one, failure in school, or financial problems. It also may occur for no apparent reason, when everything in life seems to be running smoothly.

Many people struggle with depression during the winter holiday season. People with seasonal affective disorder become depressed because of the decrease in sunlight during short winter days.

Biochemical changes in the brain, family history, personality, and the stresses of life all are significant in the development of depression. Exactly how these causes interact is not known. Depression may be more likely for some people than for others, but no one is immune. Depression is an illness that can happen to anyone at any time in life.

How to get help

When you—or a family member or friend—have symptoms of depression:

- See your doctor. Your family doctor or a doctor at a clinic can perform a thorough examination and run laboratory tests to rule out other illnesses that may cause symptoms of depression.
- Be open and honest about your feelings. Depression can be difficult to diagnose because it affects people in so many different ways. Talk about headaches, tiredness, eating problems, whatever you are experiencing. Be sure to tell your doctor that you think you are depressed.
- Get a referral for ongoing help. Your doctor may prescribe an antidepressant medication. He or she can also direct you to a therapist experienced in treating depression. Psychiatrists, psychologists, social workers, and other counselors all can provide help.
- A psychiatrist is best equipped to treat depression. As a medical doctor and counselor, a psychiatrist can perform a thorough physical and psychological evaluation, prescribe and carefully monitor the effects of medication, and provide psychotherapy.

- If you are unable to get a referral to a psychiatrist, contact the nearest university-affiliated hospital or a hospital with a psychiatric clinic. Medical staff there will be able to direct you to help. There are several national depression helplines listed at the end of this book, or you can call your state psychiatric society for a referral.
- Make a change. If you—or a family member or friend—have been in treatment for depression for more than 3 months and feel no relief, you may need a different form of treatment or a different counselor. Try to get a referral to a psychiatrist who specializes in treating mood disorders.

How is depression treated?

Today, depression can be successfully treated with a variety of antidepressant medications, various forms of psychotherapy, or some combination of these or other treatments. Your doctor will choose the best treatment plan for you or your loved one.

Antidepressants

Antidepressant drugs are the main medications used to treat depressive mood disorders. There are four types of antidepressants that work in different ways to correct a chemical imbalance in the brain.

Nine out of ten people who have depression can be helped by antidepressant medication. However, which type of medication works best varies from person to person. You may need to try several before your doctor finds the best drug for you.

It is important to understand that, though these drugs are powerful in the treatment of depression, they are not addictive. Antidepressants do not provide an unnatural high and are not intended to change your personality. When taken by a healthy, nondepressed person, they have no noticeable effect.

Before taking an antidepressant, it is important to tell your doctor about any other medication you may be taking and carefully follow his or her instructions about diet, other drugs, and alcohol.

The following four categories of antidepressant drugs differ in their side effects, with the newer drugs usually causing fewer problems. Side effects can include dry mouth, drowsiness, constipation, headaches, nausea, nervousness, and insomnia. If you have side effects that last for more than a few weeks, tell your doctor. He or she may be able to adjust the dose or prescribe a different drug.

Tricyclic antidepressants (TCAs) These drugs alter the balance in the brain of the neurotransmitters (chemical messengers) norepinephrine and serotonin. Some TCAs are imipramine hydrochloride, amitriptyline hydrochloride, desipramine hydrochloride, and nortriptyline hydrochloride.

Monoamine oxidase inhibitors (MAOIs) These drugs slow the breakdown in the brain of the neurotransmitters (chemical messengers) norepinephrine and serotonin, letting them assist brain cells in sending messages for longer periods. When taking MAOIs, you must follow a special diet to avoid problems; follow your doctor's advice on which foods to avoid.

MAOI drugs include phenelzine sulfate and tranylcypromine sulfate.

Selective serotonin-reuptake inhibitors (SSRIs) These drugs work by blocking the neurotransmitter (chemical messenger) serotonin. By not interfering with other chemical messengers, SSRIs treat depression without causing the serious side effects often associated with TCAs and MAOIs.

SSRI drugs include fluoxetine hydrochloride, sertraline hydrochloride, and paroxetine.

New-generation antidepressants Two newer drugs for depression are venlafaxine hydrochloride and nefazodone hydrochloride. Venlafaxine hydrochloride blocks the neurotransmitters (chemical messengers) serotonin and norepinephrine but does not interfere with other chemical messengers (and so has few side effects). Nefazodone hydrochloride works at two locations to increase the amount of serotonin available; it also has few side effects.

Not an overnight cure As a rule, antidepressant medications must be taken for 4 to 6 weeks before thcy begin to cause substantial improvements in a depressed person's mood. Finding the right antidepressant at exactly the right dosage is likely to involve a brief period of trial and adjustment.

Often when a combination of drugs and psychotherapy will be used, a doctor will prescribe antidepressants and other necessary drugs immediately, easing the depression to help make psychotherapy more successful once it begins.

Antidepressant medications have been used safely by children under a doctor's close supervision, although they are not currently recommended for use by children. Though few problems with immediate side effects of antidepressant drugs have been reported, long-term effects of these drugs on children are not yet known. Whether to give antidepressant medications to a child must be carefully considered by the doctor and the child's parents.

Other drugs

Sometimes, an antianxiety medication or a mild tranquilizer may be prescribed along with the antidepressant medication at first to help curb the troublesome symptoms of depression. Occasionally lithium or other drugs may be taken with an antidepressant to bring about or enhance a therapeutic effect.

Hospitalization

At the start of treatment a person who has depression may be hospitalized for a brief period. Hospitalization can be used to ensure that the depressed person does not harm him- or herself or others. It also provides the doctor with an opportunity to monitor drug levels closely and adjust medical therapy.

Electroconvulsive therapy (ECT)

In rare cases where major depression deepens despite treatment with both drugs and psychotherapy, ECT may sometimes be used. ECT sends a low-level electrical signal through the brain to induce a 30- to 60-second general seizure. The result is almost always quick relief (1 to 2 weeks) from depression. ECT is then followed by treatment with antidepressant medication and psychotherapy.

Today's ECT is nothing like the crude shock treatments of the past. The electrical currents used are much lower and patients are sedated and do not feel pain during the procedure. However, temporary memory loss is a possible side effect, so careful consideration should always be given before choosing ECT.

Phototherapy

Some depressions, particularly those that are seasonal in nature, may respond to treatment with specially designed bright light therapy.

Psychotherapy

Psychotherapy or talk therapy can be very effective in treating depression. Psychotherapy may be used alone or in combination with drug treatment. During psychotherapy, a psychiatrist, psychologist, or other trained counselor talks with the depressed person about his or her feelings and experiences and helps him or her to find ways to overcome the mood disorder.

Psychotherapy alone (without drug treatment) is most successful in treating mild to moderate depression. Therapy sessions continue for about 3 to 6 months, depending on the needs of the individual. The following types of psychotherapy are used to treat depression:

Cognitive behavioral therapy In this form of talk therapy, the therapist helps a person to recognize his or her own negative thought patterns and behaviors and to replace them with positive ones. The depressed person shares his or her thoughts and problems with the therapist. This form of treatment can be used to quickly bring important changes to the depressed person's daily life and outlook for the future.

Interpersonal therapy This form of therapy focuses on the problems a person has in his or her personal and social relationships. The therapist helps the depressed person review how he or she interacts with other people, then works on how to change that behavior to improve relationships. By learning to deal more effectively with other people, the person with depression can stop creating conflict in his or her life and gain support from family and friends.

Psychodynamic therapy In this form of treatment, the therapist helps a depressed person look inside him- or herself to uncover and understand emotional conflicts that may be causing his or her depression. This is often long-term therapy that involves looking back at unresolved problems from childhood and attempting to work them out.

When it isn't depression

Many symptoms of depression can be caused by other conditions that require attention and treatment. A long list of medical conditions such as multiple sclerosis, stroke, hypothyroidism, heart disease, and cancer can produce symptoms of depression. When depression occurs along with another medical problem, both conditions must be treated. Also, reactions to some medications, exposure to a toxin (poison), or drug or alcohol abuse can resemble depression.

A complete medical examination, including a health history, laboratory tests, and a psychological evaluation, can help determine what type of help the person needs. However, depression is more difficult to diagnose when another health problem is present. If you think depression may be a part of your problem, be sure to tell your doctor.

Help yourself— or a friend

Once a person gets treatment, there are plenty of things you can do to help speed recovery from depression and help keep depression from returning. Look over the list below, then check with local hospitals, clinics, the YMCA, and other community organizations for help.

- Reduce stress. Look at your life honestly. Be realistic about what you can handle. Cut back. Give yourself a break here and there.
- Learn stress management techniques. Stress is everywhere and you can't avoid it all. Learning how to live with necessary stress can make the difference between depression and happiness.
- Set realistic, reachable goals. Celebrate small victories along the way to a big success.
- Exercise. Join a class, ride a bike, take a walk, go dancing, go outside, and get into a healthy new routine.

- Get nutritional counseling and learn to enjoy healthy eating. Depression has a way of destroying good eating habits and damaging good health.
- Socialize. Push yourself to go out more often. See friends, see a movie, eat out.

To help a friend:

- Offer your friend reassurance. A depressed person needs to hear that there is hope, that things will get better with time and effort.
- Encourage your friend to get help.
- Listen and talk openly about the depression. Let your friend tell you how he or she feels. Accept his or her feelings and be willing to talk about them.
- Compliment and encourage your friend. If you have good things to say, this is the time to say them.
- Don't criticize or judge your friend. A depressed person already feels very bad about him- or herself. Don't add to those feelings.
- Smile, hold hands, hug a lot. Affection can go right to the heart and give real comfort.
- Don't be easily pushed away. Depressed people may lash out at the people around them. Stick by your friend, no matter what happens.
- Encourage your friend to go out. Take him or her to a restaurant or a movie. Even going for walks together is a step in the right direction.

Facts and figures

Depression can occur at any time in life. Statistics tell us that:

- About 17.5 million Americans currently have some form of depression.
- About 35 million Americans living now will have moderate to severe depression at some time in their lives.
- About 10 percent of all American adults are diagnosed with depression each year.
- About 10 percent of all children under 13 and about 5 to 10 percent of all adolescents are clinically depressed.
- Women are more than twice as likely as men to seek help and receive a diagnosis of clinical depression.
- The first episode of depression occurs early in life, typically during adolescence or young adulthood.
- It is estimated that untreated depression costs American employers as much as $43 billion per year through sick days, lost productivity, employee turnover, and medical bills.

Women vs men

The traditional view in our society is that women are far more likely to be depressed and are more likely to seek help for depression. In 1970, statistics showed that women in the United States were three times as likely as men to be diagnosed with clinical depression. However, in the 1980s, the difference dropped to 2.4 women to every man receiving medical treatment for depression. More recent statistics on treatment for depression show women leading men by a ratio of 1.7 to 1.

Is depression more common among women? As children, boys and girls appear equally susceptible to depression. However, once children become sexually mature adults, women take the lead. This suggests that hormonal changes or gender roles may play a part in triggering depression.

In our society, it has always been acceptable for women to express their feelings, while men were expected to keep their feelings inside. Under these conditions, women were more likely to acknowledge the problem and seek help for depression; men would tend to deny the problem or refuse to get help.

Symptoms of depression in men may not always be obvious. In our culture, depression in men is sometimes expressed in terms of silent withdrawal, alcohol and drug abuse, even violence.

Why are the numbers of men increasing? Depression is an illness that is affecting more people than ever before in general, and more men than ever before in particular. Changing gender roles, job layoffs and downsizing, and the aging of baby boomers add up to more people who are more susceptible to depression. At the same time, the changing roles of men and women in society may be making it easier for men to seek help for depression rather than keeping their feelings hidden.

What is a nervous breakdown?

Most of us have heard of a person having a nervous breakdown. What does this mean? "Nervous breakdown" is a popular term sometimes used to describe what has happened to a person who has a major depression. When a depression is severe enough to prevent the person from functioning normally in daily life, or when the symptoms of depression appear suddenly, it may seem as if the person has "broken down."

With appropriate diagnosis and treatment of depression, the person can get well and start enjoying life again.

How long does depression last?

A depression can last days, weeks, months, or a lifetime. Some people have a brief depression, recover, and the problem never returns. Others have bouts of major depression throughout their lives. And some people never recover from a mild depression.

Depression is usually a recurring disease. After one episode of depression, a person has a 50 percent likelihood of having another within 5 years. After three episodes, the odds go up to 90 percent that depression will return again.

The sooner depression is diagnosed and treated, the better. Left untreated, a mild episode of depression can progress into a major depression; a few bothersome symptoms can grow into a disabling condition. A person can overcome an episode of depression without any help, but it generally takes much longer—up to 1 1/2 years—and the risk of a return episode is greater.

How dangerous is depression?

Depression is a whole body disorder that can cause "whole life" problems. The disabling moods of depression can damage a person's marriage, family relationships and friendships, job performance, and health. The longer a depression is allowed to continue, the more the damage is spread.

A major depression can cause a person to shut him- or herself off from the love and support of friends and family or strike out violently, verbally and physically attacking others.

Most threatening is the connection between depression and suicide. It is estimated that 15 percent of all people who have a major depression will take their own lives. Prompt treatment and continuing support for a person with depression can mean the difference between life and death.

Suicide warning signs

After a person commits suicide, family and friends may realize that there were warning signs they missed. Learn to look for these warning signs and get help right away if you suspect someone you know is considering suicide. Watch for:

- Talk about suicide or death. About 80 percent of people who kill themselves talk about suicide before taking action.
- Writings or drawings about suicide. This clue is often presented by children and adolescents.
- A failed suicide attempt. Many people who successfully take their own lives do so after one or more failed attempts. Any suicide attempt is a call for help.
- Puzzling comments. Sayings such as "Things will be different soon," "You won't have to worry about me much longer," or "All this will be over soon" may refer to planning suicide.
- Impulsive, reckless behavior. Taking big chances and casually risking injury may reveal a wish for death.
- Drug or alcohol abuse. Alcohol consumption is involved in up to 50 percent of all successful suicides.

- Putting things in order and tying up loose ends. An adult may get all his or her business affairs in order, revise a will, check the insurance, pay bills off. A child may catch up on all of his or her schoolwork.
- Giving away treasured objects. A person planning suicide may give away favorite possessions. Both adults and children do this.
- Saying goodbye. A person planning suicide may contact relatives or old friends one more time before taking action.
- Making a plan and getting the tools ready. A person contemplating suicide may plan ahead. For example, he or she may buy a gun or hoard prescription drugs.
- A sudden good mood—even happiness. A very depressed person, once having decided on a plan to commit suicide, may feel relief.

Special alert: Suicide is most likely to occur when it seems that the threat has passed. Many people who have been struggling through a major depression will kill themselves when things seem to be getting better, 2 or 3 months into recovery. For some very depressed people, this may be the first time they have had enough emotional energy to act. Others may be overwhelmed by the problems depression has caused.

Suicide prevention: what to do

- Watch for warning signs.
- Never ignore talk about suicide, no matter how unlikely it seems.
- Get medical help immediately. Call 911. Call your doctor or psychiatrist.
- If you think the person may harm him- or herself, stay close by until help arrives. Don't leave the person alone.
- Go to the nearest hospital emergency department as soon as possible. Don't wait until the person attempts suicide. Major depression is a dangerous disease and medical personnel are trained to deal with it.

Who is at risk for depression?

Everyone is at risk. There are stressful events in every part of life that can lead to depression. For example:

- A neglected infant can become listless and refuse to eat.

- A new mother may have postpartum blues that last indefinitely.
- Working women and men deal daily with family- and job-related stresses that can trigger depression.
- People who are seriously ill often find their health problems compounded by depression.

It is reassuring to know that most people, especially when they have the love and support of family and friends, are able to handle stress, recover in a short time, and enjoy life again.

Groups particularly at risk

Three specific groups that appear to have particular difficulty battling depression are children, adolescents, and older people.

Young children

Though depression generally first appears in the teen years or during adulthood, no one is too young to be depressed.

A newborn whose mother is inattentive may become depressed and stop eating or developing normally (this is called "failure to thrive"). Depressed children as young as 5 years old have committed suicide.

Because we often think of childhood as a happy, carefree time of life, some of us may mistakenly consider children to be immune to depression. As many as 10 percent of children under age 13 may be depressed. Research has shown that the younger a child is when he or she has a first depression, the more likely that child is to have recurrent episodes of depression throughout life.

Even a mild depression can cause a child to have low self-esteem and make childhood's business of making friends and learning to get along with others very difficult. The sooner a depression is discovered and treated, the sooner a child can get back to "feeling like a kid" again.

Children are naturally joyful beings. A child may not understand his or her own feelings of depression or know the words to express those feelings. Often, depressed children just say they are sad or they may complain of headaches or stomachaches. A child may have depression when he or she:

- looks sad most of the time and never smiles or laughs
- frequently reports feeling sad, bored, or sick
- is negative and pessimistic
- isn't cheered by happy events or fun activities
- walks with "heavy" legs or reports having no energy
- has trouble in school or with friends

- is unusually irritable
- has sleep problems or frequent nightmares
- talks about death or about hurting him- or herself

If such symptoms continue for 2 weeks or more, take your child to see his or her doctor and ask for a referral to a child psychiatrist. Your doctor will rule out any medical conditions or the possibility of abuse, which can also cause depression, then help determine the best course of treatment.

Psychotherapy designed to help a child learn positive thinking habits at an early age can head off years of unhappiness. Children who can think positively can lighten a current depression and possibly prevent future episodes. Psychotherapy may include family counseling or therapy.

A simple, gentle backrub performed by a parent for 30 minutes a day also can help depressed children to feel happier and less anxious, and enable them to sleep better. Research shows that such a massage, and the parent-child closeness it promotes, can improve the balance of chemicals (neurotransmitters) in the brain. Hugs help, too.

Antidepressants are also sometimes used to treat depression in children. Drugs used successfully to treat adults often work differently on children's still developing minds and bodies. Although these drugs can sometimes speed recovery from depression, their use in treating children is still under investigation and should be carefully considered.

Teenagers

The teenage years are tough times. The trip from childhood to adulthood is filled with emotional ups and downs, new challenges, and new concerns. As teenagers begin to mature, it is normal for them to be moody and to have feelings of frustration, anger, and sadness.

Depression in teenagers, however, is not normal—but it is all too common. It is estimated that 5 to 10 percent of all teenagers have depression or manic-depressive illness.

With professional help, teenagers can overcome depression and prevent its recurrence. But less than half of all adolescents with depression will get professional help.

Depression in teenagers is always a cause for concern. Suicide is the third leading cause of death among teenagers, after accidents and homicide. And if you consider the role depression plays in many accidental deaths involving alcohol or driving, the number of depression-related deaths rises dramatically.

Even when there is no threat of suicide, depression causes eating disorders and self-destructive habits that can lead to serious lifelong health problems. Also, studies show that as many as 55 percent of depressed teens turn to alcohol or drugs in an attempt to self-medicate, making matters worse.

Teenagers who have depression may simply say they're sad. While they feel all the frustration, isolation, and other symptoms that depressed adults describe, they may not fully understand their feelings or know how to describe them.

Teenagers may not talk about their depression, but it will show in their expression, body language, and behavior.

Teenagers are famous for bad attitudes. A teenager will rebel, sulk, stomp around the house, or slam the door to his or her room. How can you tell the difference between normal teenage behavior and real depression?

Adolescents are moody, but when a teenager is sad—or irritable, anxious, negative, or uncooperative—for more than 2 weeks, a parent should talk to the child about his or her feelings and seek professional help.

Review the general list of symptoms of depression early in this book. Consider also these warning signs of depression in a teenager:

- looks different and worse than usual—with dirty hair, dirty clothes, or an exceptionally messy room

- does badly in school—gets lower grades or cuts classes
- drops out of favorite activities such as music or sports or stops getting together with friends
- becomes angry, irritable, aggressive, or uncooperative without cause
- seems to sleep all the time or almost never
- begins using drugs or alcohol
- becomes sexually promiscuous
- is involved in dangerous or risky behavior
- feels guilty for no real reason
- has trouble thinking or remembering things
- withdraws from friends and family
- complains of constant headaches or stomachaches
- talks about death or about hurting him- or herself

If you suspect your teen is depressed, get help right away. Your attention to the problem can help a mildly depressed teen make a quick and complete recovery. For a seriously depressed adolescent, prompt action can mean the difference between life and death.

How to help a depressed child or teenager

- Be there. A child who is depressed needs you to be available both physically and emotionally. He or she may try to push you away, so gently but firmly insist on helping.
- Listen. Nothing you can say will matter as much as what you let your child say. Encourage your child to talk about his or her feelings. Then really listen. Loving parents may be tempted to interrupt gloomy or frightening statements with, "Don't be silly, you're the greatest kid in the world," or "You have everything going for you," or "Don't say such terrible things." Don't do it. It is very hard to hear your child say self-destructive things, but you need to know what he or she is thinking if you want to be able to help. Sad and frightening feelings have to be expressed or your child will feel more isolated. He or she will become harder to reach and help.
- Don't criticize or try to fix things. This is a learning opportunity for the parent, not the child. Don't lecture and don't expect to "make it all better" right away.
- Reassure. A depressed teen thinks the bad feelings will last forever. Help your child understand that he or she will feel better. Show that you understand his or her feelings.

Make it clear that this bad time is temporary and that you will get the help he or she needs.

- Get help. Don't hesitate. Call your pediatrician, family doctor, or a hospital with a psychiatric clinic right away. Your doctor can rule out physical problems that may be causing the symptoms of depression and can refer you to a psychiatrist or other counselor skilled in working with teenagers.
- Stay involved. Make sure your child is getting the help that he or she really needs. You may have to change counselors, or medications may need to be adjusted. Recovery may take weeks or months, and depression can recur. Learn all you can about depression so you can help make the best choices for your child and provide support at home.
- Guard against suicide. Take every self-destructive comment or action seriously. The terrible truth is that about 15 percent of all depressed teenagers commit suicide. Watch for warning signs (see Suicide warning signs) and get help immediately.

Teenage suicide—the threat is real

Depressed teenagers are in real danger of choosing a permanent solution—death—to the temporary problems they are facing. Increasing the risk is the inability of most teenagers to understand fully that death is final.

No threat of suicide by a child or adolescent, no matter how wild or crazy sounding, should ever be ignored. Even a terribly painful or gross death may look like relief to a child or adolescent who is dealing with the pain of a deep depression.

Whenever a child or teenager is depressed, friends and family must be aware of the danger of suicide. Don't be afraid to talk frankly about your child's intentions. And don't hesitate to get help.

Older people

Many older people experience loss, illness, and loneliness. And depression can sometimes make this time of life much more difficult.

Often a depression that could easily be treated and relieved is mistaken for a natural part of aging, both by the older person and by family and friends. In most cases, medical treatment can help a depressed older person return to normal.

Symptoms of depression in older people may sometimes be mistaken for symptoms of senile dementia (Alzheimer's disease). When an older person seems disoriented or distracted or has memory loss (all symptoms of senile dementia), he or she may actually be depressed.

Many health problems related to aging can cause symptoms of depression. And medications for high blood pressure, Parkinson's disease, and other medical problems common to older people can also produce symptoms similar to those caused by depression.

The rates of suicide from depression rise substantially with advancing years. The highest suicide rates are for single or widowed white males over age 55.

How to help an older person who is depressed

- Take him or her to a doctor for a thorough medical evaluation.
- Check the medicine cabinet and make sure his or her doctor knows about all of the medications—prescription and over-the-counter—the person uses.
- Be sure depression is discussed and fully considered by the doctor.
- Take him or her to therapy sessions.
- Remind him or her to take any medication as prescribed.
- Be an available friend. Be a person who calls, visits, and keeps in touch.

- Get physical. Few older people get enough physical affection. Hug often.
- Take him or her out. It won't always be easy to get him or her to go, but don't give up.
- Get him or her back into life. Help find activities, interests, or groups to brighten each day. For senior citizen activities, check churches, synagogues, or community centers.
- Know suicide warning signs and watch for them. Don't be afraid to say something or take action.

Reach out for support

Depression can make you feel lonely, but you are not alone. There are many people around you who know how it feels to be depressed and who can help you. For assistance finding medical help or support groups in your area, contact:

The National Foundation for Depressive Illness (NAFDI)
800 248-4344

NAFDI's hotline has a recorded message about depressive illnesses and helps callers receive a referral list of local support groups and doctors who specialize in treating depression. It also can provide a list of useful magazine and newspaper articles and books about depression.

The Depressive and Related Affective Disorders Association (DRADA)
410 955-4647

DRADA works in cooperation with The Johns Hopkins University School of Medicine. Like centers at many large teaching hospitals, DRADA provides a variety of outreach programs, classes, and support groups for people who have depression and their families in their area. DRADA also reaches out to people across the country to help them find help locally. Write DRADA, Meyer 3-181, 600 N Wolfe St, Baltimore, Md 21287-7381.

The National Depressive and Manic-Depressive Association (NDMDA)
800 826-3632

This association is a source of information about mood disorders.

The National Mental Health Association (NMHA)
800 969-6642

The National Institute of Mental Health's (NIMH) Depression Awareness, Recognition, and Treatment Program
800 421-4211

The National Alliance for the Mentally Ill
800 950-6264

Notes on medication